I0624118

# ENIGMA

## and Other Aromantic Asexual Love Poems

by Sophie A. Katz

ISBN: 979-8-9902297-0-9 (ebook)
ISBN: 979-8-9902297-1-6 (paperback)

Cover art by Sarah Schmidt.
Author photo by Tiffany Bagwell.

Printed in the United States of America.

First printing, 2024.

https://www.sophie-a-katz.com/

To R., K., M., A., L., and D. –
Some of these poems were for you,
but now they're for everyone.

Especially for my parents –
my first audience, my first editors,
my foremost cheerleaders.

And for my friends who keep asking
when they can buy a book of my poetry.

I love you all.

# A Few Definitions

## Aromantic
A person who experiences little-to-no
romantic attraction.
*Related terms*: "aro," "aromantic spectrum,"
"aro-spec," "a-spec," etc.

## Asexual
A person who experiences little-to-no
sexual attraction.
*Related terms*: "ace," "asexual spectrum," "ace-spec,"
"a-spec," etc.

## Greyromantic
An aromantic microlabel;
a person who experiences romantic attraction
rarely, infrequently, ambiguously,
or only under specific circumstances.
*Related terms*: "grey-aromantic," "grey-aro,"
"aromantic spectrum," "a-spec," etc.

## Demisexual
An asexual microlabel;
a person who only feels sexual attraction towards
another person after establishing an emotional bond
with that person.
*Related terms*: "demi," "grey-ace," "asexual spectrum,"
"a-spec," etc.

## Allosexual
A person who regularly experiences sexual attraction.
*Related terms*: "allo," "not asexual," etc.

# Preface

I've been going back and forth about whether to include this preface.

One of my favorite undergraduate professors, Ed Folsom, would open each discussion about the Dickinson or Whitman poem we were reading that day by asking us, the class, what it meant. If we said something he'd never thought of before, he'd *smile*.

In that class, I learned that part of the fun of poetry is seeing what the reader brings to the table.

These poems mean what they mean to me, yes. Knowing more about me and my life would shape the way you interpret these poems. At the same time, these poems will also mean what they mean to *you*. You might relate to what I've written. You might find it completely alien to your experience. And I *want* that, both of it, all of it – because of course there are areas of overlap in our experiences, and there are also points where I must put my foot down and say, "No! This is different! I need you to see that it's different, and that that's not a bad thing!"

You're going to have a unique perspective on this book. Yes, there are things that I hope you will think about it. However, if I tell you what I hope you will think, that might alter your perspective.

On the other hand... isn't that part of the point of writing? To alter the reader's perspective?

What I will say is this:

A part of me hopes that when you looked at the cover of this book and read the phrase, "aromantic asexual love poems," you thought, "Isn't that a contradiction?"

Because then I would get to say, "Sure it is, and at the same time, it's real. These concepts are supposed to be incompatible, but they all exist in me, and I'm real. And we're set up by the world we live in to find that confusing – to think that such a contradiction is a problem to overcome, a puzzle to solve, an enigma. So we *feel* that it is all those things. It *has been* all those things.

"But it doesn't have to be."

# Contents

# Enigma

A single night has passed, and you have gone
Away from where you lived inside my heart –
And I've forgotten what it's like to want you.

I lie here in the darkness, reaching out
For hunger that I know will cause me pain,
But still I cannot grasp or bring it in me.
Still I cannot find it, not within me.

A single day since I no longer love you,
And every inch of me no longer loves you.
Attraction gone as quickly as it came,
Attraction lost as quickly as a text,

And this demisexual, left behind, perplexed –

With this enigma:
For you were once so much, so much of me –
Not long ago at all, so much of me –
How can you be nothing to me now?

Two nights ago, I savored every thought of you.
Two nights ago, I quivered at the touch of you.
Two nights ago, I smoldered deep within for you.

Tonight, it's like I never did at all.

And if wanting you can vanish so completely,
What else from you can vanish so completely?

I didn't know how quick my heart could rush
At thought of one; your presence showed me that.
I didn't know how close someone could seem
Though far away; your nearness taught me that.

I didn't know what love songs really meant
Or that I'd ever sing them, and yet I sang to you.
I didn't know what pleasure fingers brought,
And yet I came to learn, with encouragement from
  you.

And now –

I reach for you not out of warm desire,
But out of fear of losing all those things –
Those happy things, those shining things, love's
  things –
That through my love for you I had discovered.

But all those things that I through you discovered –

THEY ARE IN ME.

And though you're gone, I find them still within me.
This heart, my power to love, is still within me.
This voice, my power to share it – still within me.
This touch, my power to pleasure – still within me.

These powers are not lost to me, as you are.
This goodness has not fled from me, as you have.

2

My self is mine to keep, and mine to hold,
And mine to choose to give to someone else,
To woman, to man, to gender-boundless soul –
I'll give to them as I once gave to you,
I'll get from them as I once got from you,
I'll feel for them as I once felt for you,
I'll sing to them as I once sang to you,
To them to whom MY LOVE will me attract –
MY LOVE. For though it has no subject now,
My love – for whom? – is still within me, too.

# I Am Yours

I am yours to sit up with past midnight
I am yours now to hold very near
I am yours to give flowers and chocolates
I am yours when I tell you my fears

I am yours when you soothe all my worries
I am yours when I calm all your rants
I am yours when we're both being silly
I am yours since you gave me the chance

I am yours when we meet in the morning
I am yours when I tell you goodbye
I am yours, though the allos will tell us
That love without sex is a lie

# To Be Seen

To be seen

To be seen

To be seen

                is a treasure.

To be known

                is a joy.

To be held
        dear in
                your heart –

Hear –

To be heard

                is a pleasure.

                And you hear.

                And you see.

                And you know.

                And you know.

                And you know.

# Forgive Me

Forgive me for believing it was all exaggeration.
Forgive me for responding to romance with
  aggravation.

Forgive me for assuming that our brains would
  work the same.
Forgive me for how long I took to recognize the
  game.

Forgive me, for I thought my lack of passion made
  me wise.
Forgive me, for these thoughts were how I calmed
  my lonely cries.

Forgive me now for all the years I doubted what you
  feel,
And maybe I'll forgive you now, for saying I'm not
  real.

# This Hand is Yours

This hand is yours
for as long as you would like it to be

This hand is yours
for as long as you want it
for as long as you need it
for as long as our fingers fit so well together
in that space between our sides

This hand is yours
for as long as this is right for us
for as long as togetherness
means smiles
and laughter
and late-night ice cream
and peace away from all that means us harm

That is to say
This hand is yours
for as long as yours is mine

# I Am Whole

I am whole, now, I am whole.
But there's a thing that I am not
Since yesterday
Another day
Another way of walking through the world

This night, these nights, I lie in bed,
Mind scrabbling at the edges of a sense I used to
    know.
I used to know.
I used to like it, I remember, used to want.
I used to want.
I didn't want, at first, I never did.
And then I did
And then I didn't
In a pattern I have come to know too well.

My fingers slide, now, on a surface
Where they once before found purchase.
It's too smooth, now, too ephemeral
Where once I found a grip –
But I am whole, now, I am whole, now,
I am whole.

I see infinity within me
Like the infinite hotel my father told me once about –
A paradox, to find an empty room –
And yet you can, if all the guests move one room
    down the hall.

And once a rabbi told me that when G-d first made
   the world –
For G-d was everywhere, back then,
And shrank to give the world some space
But still is everywhere and infinite.
G-d is everywhere and infinite,
And I –
I too am infinite,
In love
And lust
And not.

Right now is me,
And then is me,
And how I will be still is me,
And I am whole and multitudinous!
Am whole and multitudinous.

The allos tell me that I'm fickle,
As inconstant as the Moon –
They would scold her for her phases, hold her still –
But she's already whole.

# Us

It's better to wait, sometimes,
As fireworks fade, and smoke gives way to stars.
It's better to wait,
To introduce denim to damp concrete
At the base of Cinderella Castle's walls.

It's better to stay a little later,
To lean against his chest and watch
the once-in-a-lifetime visitors and the
    Instagrammers
fumble with phone settings and curse the lack of
    light
that ruins this opportunity for a photo with no one
    in the background –

They don't see us sitting there.

There are strangers in every picture I took with
    him,
But I don't see them.
There were thousands of people crammed around
    us moments ago –
Now cramming onto monorails and buses and boats –
But I didn't see them, either.
I'm sure I heard them sing along,
But it's hard to separate from my own voice.
I'm sure I felt their heat,
But it's hard to separate from the sweat of a Florida
    day.

I'm sure I saw them, sure I did,
But they didn't matter –
Because his arms were around me,
As they are now,
And his chin was on my shoulder,
As it is now,

And I don't think anyone can see us, here.
In the most popular theme park on Earth,
I don't feel any eyes on me.

There's only us.

# Coyotes

My father says, when I am thirteen
and I know that I am different –
"You were eight, and all the other girls
played 'Chase After the Boys,'
but you would play 'Let's Take a Trip to Mars.'"

"It was the desert," I correct him –
a stickler for such details –
"I searched for water in the desert,
and I hid from coyotes."

Whichever terrain I imagined,
earthly or alien,
My brain did not provide a prince to wed me there,
nor a princess.
(There was one inside my Playmobil set –
I put her hair on the body of the knight
so she could ride the horse and face the dragon.)

The odd thing is, it earned me praise –
both indirect and fleeting –
But it was praise, from wise adults, for this demure,
    romanceless girl
with no distractions, no desire, save a healthy love
    of books.

My coyotes came in packs –
all pale and blonde, with fang-filled smiles and
    shadowed eyes –

They found me, and they saw I was alone, and
    howled skyward:
*Tell us what you're hiding! Who's your crush?*
But I had none, and there was none to find,
no matter how they tried to claw it out of me
like water in the desert, or on Mars.

I am twenty-nine. It took me long enough
to ignore the claws and howls,
to see the water and its lack as just as good
and just as right
and just as whole.

I'm aro-spec, I know that now,
and still a stickler for such details
and so very glad I finally have the words.

# Dimensions of Love

His love was temperamental.
        Your love is warm.
Their love was conditional.
        Your love is constant.
Her love was distant.
        Your love is present.
My love is for you.
        Your love is for me.


# Four-Letter Words

To love is to care

And to care
Is to feel what's theirs

To delight in their rejoicing
And sorrow in their despair –

To open your heart
And find a second rhythm there.

# Self-Immolation

You build a bonfire to burn yourself in the name of
    lifting me up.

You crush yourself into kindling as you compliment
    my completeness.

Your breath becomes the bellows,
and your feelings feed the flames,
and you expect me to sit and sing campfire songs
while you reduce yourself to ash.

But I am not a hot air balloon.
Your pain cannot uplift me,
and, lover, I derive no warmth from your
    self-immolation.

# Perhaps I Cannot Keep You Warm

Perhaps I cannot keep you warm.
I'm willing, still, to try –
I haven't heat enough for me
When all alone I lie.

These fingers are but icy bones.
My feet are frozen, too.
A snowwoman gave me her crown –
What could I give to you?

My time, my words, my caring ear,
My heart – if you would ask.
If I could hold you through the night,
Would winter end at last?

# I Claim the Right

I claim the right to name myself,
To define my pathway, my perception,
My interaction – my attraction –
               or lack thereof.

I claim, I relate
I celebrate

And may all who hear me see
there is another way to be
               and it is good to be.

          It is good to be.

# Commitment

Commitment comes with purpose
In my heart, my deed, my head;
I have no plans to fall in love –
I'll walk on in instead.

# Leaving

How sweet it is –
I say it's so –
To love so much
You hate to go.

# Again

I'm eager for beginnings,
Though I never liked an end;
I've been in love before,
And I will fall in love again.

# I Have...

I have
eyes for stars and sunrise, and I have
ears for words and music, and I have
lungs for belly-laughing, and I have
hands for puppy petting, and I have
legs for crossing mountains, and I have
arms for hugs and holds

and I have
webs of friends and family, and I have
worlds of my creation, and I have
games of joy and challenge, and I have
poems of inspiration, and I have
dreams of every future, and I have
time of my own to spend

and I have
happiness in triumph, and I have
sorrow in disaster, and I have
worry in my failings, and I have
pride in all my work, and I have
fury in injustice, and I have
gratitude for all

*but she lacks*
*romantic*
*attraction*

*what a foolish little card shark*
*to forget that hearts are trump*

# Labels

I went into the grocery store one day,
And there were no labels.
All the fruit was mixed up on the shelves,
The apples and the oranges combined
With lemons, pumpkins, avocadoes, limes...
I asked for a banana, and they said,
Just take one. Isn't every fruit the same?
Everybody eats their fruit the same, and likes the
    same,
And everybody needs the same nutrition,
So why make a fuss and ask for something
    different?
Why make our day more difficult by asking for
    bananas?

I went into the library one day,
And there were no labels.
So I said, which shelf has fantasy?
And they said, why does it matter?
Every book's the same, you know,
And every reader is the same.
Who would need something specific?
Why should you want something different?
Can't you get along with everyone,
Enjoy whatever book you find?
Why waste our time with made-up problems,
Unless you're trying to be a problem?

I went into the world the other day,
And I had no labels
Because everyone's the same in all the world,
Or so they said,
Every body wants the same thing in the world,
Or so they said,
And if you think you might be different, then you're
  wrong,
Or so they said

So take these words and they will fix you,
Take these pills and they will fix you,
Take this dick and it will fix you,

And if they cannot fix you, shut your mouth,
Cause you're the only one who has a problem.
You're the only one, so You're the problem.
You are all alone

And that's the problem...

I go into the world today, and I have my labels,
And I will never be the only one again,
And I will never be convinced I am alone again.

# Promises
*a Tanka*

We make promises:
to bring each other joy, and
to hold each other
foremost in our hearts as we
build a future together.


# Friendship
*a Tanka*

I carry inside
my mouth, the things you would say;
inside my mind, the
memories made together;
inside my chest, your heartbeat.

# Ever After

There's another ever after
    tucked away between the pages
    of the storybooks they read to you
    and in between the frames of all the films.

There's another kind of ending
    and it's more like a beginning –
    Can you see it in my smile? Do you
    understand that I'm already whole?

There's another kind of happy
    found in friendship, found in family,
    found in music played and sung, and found
    in petting dogs and staring at the clouds.

There's another way of living
    and I found it, and I love it,
    and I've found a million like me –
    found the aces, found the demis, found the
      greys.

This is happy ever after
    in simplicity and details,
    in a spectrum, in identity,
    in knowing who I am and how I love.

# Around My Heart

If you could put your hand around my heart,
What would you do with it?

Hold it? With caution, or with care?
Tap it? Confuse me with an extra beat?
Squeeze it? Restrict me, or constrict me?

You already can, I think, you already have –
Every breath, every step – you are inside of me,

And I don't know what to do with you.

# Comets

Two comets shared a galaxy
Though soared on different paths
Through stars and planets, til the day
Their orbits chanced to pass

In coming near, their journeys changed
As gravity took hold
They spun together through the void
With tails of white and gold

These icy dancers travel still –
I watch them here from home –
The sparkling trails that they create
Could not be made alone

# No Longer Do
*a Villanelle*

I needed you.
But all the thoughts that made me smile
no longer do.

In hindsight, I had every clue.
I ignored the growing pile –
I needed you.

I thought what left our lips stood true,
but songs which once could cross the miles
no longer do.

I face a day uncertain, new,
without the guide I had then, while
I needed you.

My mind is dwelling now, as minds will do,
on all the things we did, and I'll
no longer do.

What's done is done. And I've a different view.
Your touch, a source of joy, I now revile...
I needed you.
No longer do.

# Starlight

I gave my light to a black hole
I opened, let him see my soul

I gladly gave, I let him take
He gladly took, all for his sake

And this was love, I thought, was told,
To put him first, to have, to hold

I never saw it as a lack
That never once did he give back...

Now, lucky me, I see things clearer,
And I will give my light to mirrors

To those who, opening to me,
Reflect my light for all to see.

# Moonlight

I thought I was the Moon, my love.

Poor Moon, who loiters in the sky
And casts reflected silver on the earth;

Cold Moon, who works with light she's lent,
Who glows through her proximity
To one who shines with golden warmth.

I thought I was the Moon, my love,
And saw in you the Sun...

But now I know – the Sun's a single star,
And I

Am just as warm
And just as bright
As you could ever shine.

# Gardening

Love is not the absence of argument
but the presence of those
who would do the dirty work
of removing the weeds
to allow the flowers

to breathe

# Possible Love

I am in love with possibility.
I pick flowers for what-ifs,
and I give jewelry to maybes.
I take somedays on dates,
and I buy boxes of chocolates for hopes.
I stare deep into the eyes of wishes
as hand in hand, we walk beside the sea...

I am in love, you see, with possibility,
with lack of guarantee,
with hasn't happened yet, but could
but would
*but really should.*

It really should be *you* I give the chocolates,
and the flowers,
and the jewelry, earrings colorful and funny-shaped
   and cheap,
until we can afford to
would decide to
*will agree*
to link our hearts with golden rings
for all to see.

It should be your hand, your eyes,
our walk, our lives,
our way
on a date at the seashore
someday.

# HeartBroke
*a Specular Poem*

I broke
Open my heart
To make room for someone else. Why
Should it hurt me if I failed
To keep him?
Should it hurt me if I failed
To make room for someone else? Why
Open my heart?
I broke.

# Enchained

I want to be an obligation.
I want to be a chain upon your wrists,
unshakable, unbreakable –

And I want to be enchained by you.
The ties that bind are roots that nourish me,
as though I were a metal tree –

It may sound cold.
But I have no desire to be free,
when I am holding you, and you are holding me.

# We Fly

We fly
Across the miles
On wings of electricity
And thought

We trace
Invisible pathways
Sending purple hearts and golden grins
By text

My heart
Desires to send my hands
(And feet, and legs, and head)
(And love)
To you

# Nothing and Everything

It's the sneaking suspicion that everyone else is making it all up, or at least exaggerating.

It's expecting nothing and expecting everything.

It's years and years prioritizing *should want* over *want* before I noticed, before I realized, before I learned. Before I had the words to learn.

It's theory of mind – recognizing my own senses, my own experience, as separate from others'.

It's knowing that what I see as *blue* and what you see as *blue* might be two different things and being fine with it.

It's a truth beyond *we're all the same*, because we're not, and we should be fine with it.

It's certainty in uncertainty and it's stability in inconstancy.

It's taking off the blinders and putting on the fuzzy slippers.

It's cozy blankets and cuddly cats and a book I love in my lap.

It's a kind of wholeness, a sense of my own completeness, unmatched by any sense in the world.

It's expecting nothing and expecting everything.

It's seeing myself everywhere that no one meant to represent me.

It's seeing myself when he doesn't have time for romance, when she sticks out her tongue at the thought of kissing someone, when they manage to escape the film without getting paired up in the end.

It's *I'm not an alien, please stop saying I'm not human, please stop saying that these feelings are what make us human.*

It's *I'm not a robot* and *I'm not a mythical creature* but it's also *robots are cool* and *people say I don't exist, too.*

It's trying on labels and trying on labels and thinking and thinking and overthinking and being told *you're making a hasty decision; you don't know that it will* never *happen.*

It's being too much and not enough. I am always too much and not enough. I am always expecting nothing and expecting everything.

It's wondering if I will ever feel safe with a straight person.

It's wondering if I will ever feel safe with a queer person.

It's wondering if I will ever feel safe on a date, or in your room, or in my skin.

It's wondering if I want what you want, or if you want what I want, and if your feelings will change when I tell you.

It's expecting nothing and expecting everything.

It's *but that's just how everyone is* and *you just haven't found the right person yet* and *you'll understand when you're older*, but it isn't, and I won't, and I already do.

It's *don't give up* and *don't lose hope* and *don't close yourself off to possibilities* and don't you get it, I finally found it, I'm finally comfortable with myself in a way I never knew was possible!

It's knowing that I am nothing and that I am everything.

It's looking at all the ways I've grown and changed and flourished and accomplished and wondering why this one, *this one*, makes me a late bloomer.

It's dragons and gryphons and space and cake and garlic bread and playing cards.

It's a waste of time.

It's giving myself permission to waste my time.

It's giving myself permission to spend my time on things I like and actions I value and people who mean something to me in a way that doesn't lead to marriage.

It's knowing that there's no such thing as wasted time, that I *have* time, and that I get to decide.

It's discovering the difference between want and need and can and must and should and might and will.

It's finding people who expect nothing and everything.

It's feeling safe with the people who expect nothing and everything.

It's a gift from me to me, or from G-d to me, or from my mother to me, and I may choose to share it.

It's a gift from me to me, or from Tumblr to me, or from my father to me, and I might not choose to share it.

It's love, and it's not love, and it's what love means to me, to me, to me.

It's *I'm not an alien, but on* Star Trek, *they tell Mister Spock that these feelings are what make us human.*

# You Never Asked, But...

You never asked, but I had a great day, thank you,
Because I petted a dog
And I saw a pretty cloud
And I made a little kid smile

You never asked, but my favorite color is blue
And my favorite food is pasta
And I love elephants and fairy tales
And anything that's soft and huggable

You never asked, but I wanted to work with you
And to write with you
And to build a future together with you
And to be asked to build a future together with you

You never asked, but I would have liked it if you'd
    asked
About my day, about my favorites,
About the future that I wanted

But you never asked.

# Out of Love

There is no falling out of love

There's only time
And growth
And all the things you never knew a person was
(until they grew too noisy to ignore)

If I lay down on a surgeon's table, she would find
a puzzle
deep inside me –
all the pieces of myself that I still dedicate to you
and you
and you
and all the yous I've consciously forgotten
until words
(and thoughts)
(and sparks)
remind me

There is no falling out of love

Love is good
and love is always good
and love that was
was
good

Most loves will end,
but none can be undone.

# Date More

My momma thinks that I
Should date more
Because
I need to learn more –
what I want
what I need
and what
I'm willing to put up with

But I think that I
Have learned a lot already
Because
I've loved and lost
and each time I redraw the line
and I say, *I deserve better*
and I say,
*never again*

(and still I say, *again, again, again*)

# Missing You

it sticks with me / how much I miss you

it whispers in my ears / where your voice
  should be
and it stares into my eyes / where your gaze
  should be
and it slides between my fingers / where your hand
  should be
and it rests against my shoulder / where your head
  should be

it keeps me company / how much I miss you
it fills the space /
                    / I count the days
                    / until you drive this interloper
                    / away

# To Not Believe

Possibility intoxicates me,
and stories start with "once upon a time"
and end with matrimony ever after,
or at least a kiss,
or at least
a promise
that there's a man inside the beast,
or a princess in the tower,
or a human on the other side of the world,
at the other end of the text –
all this to say that
sometimes we fall in love with ideas,
not people,
but I think it would be worse
to not believe.

# Who Raises the Dead

In Judaism, there is a prayer for everything –
for when you lie down, and when you rise up,
and when you eat, and drink, and use the restroom,

and the prayer you say when you meet someone
you haven't seen in over a year –
Blessed are you, Adonai our God,
*mechayeh hameitim* – who raises the dead.

And I think there's something dead between us,
now the Earth's gone fully round the Sun
since the first time I texted you,
and I've had more than a year of knowing you
and liking you
and loving you
and never having met you at all.

There's something in the two of us that could be
    brought to life
if only we could find the time and space to create it,
to shape it out of clay and put the breath of life
    inside of it
and care for it
with patience
and with kindness
and with trust.

We could raise the dead together,
link our hands and hearts and build
the kind of future I have prayed for –
where I am yours, and you are mine.

# Too Good

The worst person I ever loved once told me that I
 was *too good to be real*,
and I didn't know then how to wrap my tongue
 around words that would explain
why it hurt me to hear it.

I wanted to say, *but I am real*.
I wanted to say, *I choose it, you know, I choose to be
 good*.
I wanted to say, *you could choose it, too. I wish you
 would*.
*I wish you would*.

And I wonder –
when the worst person I ever loved works their way
 to my waking brain –
I wonder if they would have heard me, had I said it,
or if *good* would remain as impossible to imagine
as I was impossible to imagine.
I wonder if they ever could have seen us as the
 same.

There are two kinds of people in the world:
those who believe that there are two kinds of
 people in the world,
and me.

# The Tree Is Loved

The tree is loved
For its fragrance and flowers in spring,
And in summer it is loved
For the fruit its green leaves cradle,
And in fall, those leaves wither,
Yet still it stands loved, depicted in art
For its reds and browns and oranges
And the sparkling ice that soon follows.

As a sapling, it is loved
By the bird who nests and the child who climbs,
And as it dies, as it lies in the dirt,
It is loved by bug and hiker alike.

Might I be such a thing,
To be loved in all my colors,
In all my changes,
And in every stage of my life.

# Faults

i am selfish
i am needy, i am greedy
i stay up too late, i procrastinate
i hyperfixate – i fail to communicate –
let me elaborate:
i over-imagine, i am my own assassin
i shout, i doubt, i force myself to go without
i bow out – i stay in
i destroy my skin
i ignore my pain, i soil and stain,
i delay
i delay
and at my lowest, i claim, "i'm okay"

and i love me anyway

# Kintsugi

You are not the hand that broke you
Nor the cracks that fracture
You
Are the gold that fills the cracks
And all the work
And all the artistry and care
That you – and all who love you – took
To put it there

Our strength comes not from the breaking
But from the holding together

# Wedding Vows

*Ani l'dodi v'dodi li* –
I am my beloved's, and my beloved is mine –

And I think my parents' wedding video ruined me
  for *Mamma Mia*.

It made no sense to me, her desire to be *given away* –
By a man she'd never met, and never loved,
And why she had to ask her mom to walk her down
  the aisle –
Why was that a question?
And what made her a *gift*, for a man to take?

At my parents' wedding, *kala* and *chatan* –
Bride and groom –
Were each escorted by their loved ones down the
  aisle
As they freely walked into their partnership.
None were given. Nothing taken
But responsibility
For the future they would build together
As each other's.

I am not a gift to be given.
I want to be someone's beloved,
And for that same someone to be mine.

# To Be Loved

All I've ever loved live on
      As handprints on my mind
      As they were, who they were
         When I loved them

And those who died
And those who left
And those I never had at all –

        Does it matter?

        I loved them.

And the them they were, before the end –
      however it ended
      however they changed, or I

I still love.
I will love.

I love who they no longer are, and so they still exist
      And always will

For to be loved is to exist beyond;

To be loved is to live on.

# Queering

But it's not about love! You know that, right?
It's not about love at all.

I should have said, I meant to say,
It's not *just* about love,
And it's not about how everybody loves the same,
Because we don't.

And that's the point. You know that, right?
We're not the same, and that's the point of Pride.

We didn't fit inside the box, we never did,
Although we thought we could
(*we thought we had to*)
(*where else was there to be, except the box*)

I love the thought of *queering*, as a verb.
Of making strange,
Of bending lines,
Of warping what you see until it's blurry
and askew
and new

Because it's blurry. It's all blurry.
Gender's blurry. So is sex, and love, and lust –
It's all a blur, for me.

And I love certainty.

And I am most certain
That I am uncertain.

You will not find solid ground in me,
not the concrete you expected,
but an ice rink – green and purple, cold and clear,

And I take pride in it. You know that, right?
*(and you could learn to skate)*

# Goodnight Is Not Goodbye

A rock is not a river,
And the Sun is not the Moon;
A speech is not a saying,
And a book is not a tune;

A soup is not a sandwich,
And a cake is not a pie,
And goodnight is not goodbye, my love,
Goodnight is not goodbye.

A god is not a mortal,
And the future's not the past;
A child is not a grown-up,
And a first is not the last;

A shout is not a whisper,
And a howl is not a sigh,
And goodnight is not goodbye, my love,
Goodnight is not goodbye.

A rainbow's not a storm cloud,
And December isn't May;
A poem can't be everything
I'd ever want to say;

My joy is not a danger,
And my love is not a lie,
And goodnight is not goodbye, my love,
Goodnight is not goodbye.

# Good, Valid, Important

You are good.
And what you are is good.
And just as good,
And just as valid,
And as equally important now
As any other way a soul could live.

So go and live.

# Love Song

```
C           G                  F
```
I love you, you know I do, why would I deny it?
```
C                    G                      F
```
And what we do, you know it's true, though some
```
        G
```
folks might decry it.
```
C                    G                   F
```
But when an ace, finds her place, then life's like a

work of art,
```
      C       G                    C
```
And I, I love you with all of my heart!


```
C                          G                F
```
It might sound weird, to others' ears, but you and I

know better.
```
C                        G                          F
```
There's other ways, than straight and gay, for two
```
      G
```
to come together.
```
C                  G                F
```
It's mythical, and mystical, and it's real from the

start
```
      C       G                    C
```
That I, I love you, with all of my heart!

C      G       F

And I don't know, just where we'll go, but how I love

the ride,
C      G    F     G

And in our space, I feel so safe, with you here by my

side,
C         G

And if there comes a day, where I must go away,
F

and we will be apart,
   C     F       C

You'll know I loved you with all of my heart!
  C   F       C

Yes, I, I love you, with all of my heart!

*See video here:*

# Acknowledgements

I owe many thanks to my beta readers – Alex Katz, Emma Oliver, Meredith Sims, and my dad, Dr. Seth Katz – for reading and giving feedback on this collection before publication. I'd also like to thank my writer friends who offered to be my beta readers but were too busy to do it. I am nonetheless grateful for your enthusiasm!

Thank you, Sarah Schmidt, for creating the breathtaking cover art for this collection.

Thank you, Tiffany Bagwell, for taking my author photo and making me feel so at ease during the shoot. Find her on Instagram @BagwellPhotography or at https://tiffanybagwell.myportfolio.com.

Thank you, Mom, for always pushing me to put myself out there.

Thank you, Paige, for supporting and encouraging me through every step of publishing this book, even though these are all poems I wrote before we started dating. I love you!

Thank you to my siblings for showing me again and again that there really is such a thing as unconditional love, just like our parents taught us.

To the rest of my family, friends, teachers, mentors, classmates, coworkers... If I started listing your names, I would never stop. If you are reading this, and you've had any hand in my development as a queer Jewish writer – thank you.

I would like to give a shout out to Audrey, though.

Audrey Smith was the president of the University of Iowa Feminist Union when I was a freshman there. She was the first person I came out to as demisexual – the first person to congratulate me for finding a label that I felt fit me. It was Audrey who invited me to write something and perform it at the Feminist Voices Showcase. I told her I was worried about taking up space when someone "more marginalized" than me could have the opportunity instead. Audrey told me that I should do it anyway – that my story was worth telling and someone would benefit from hearing it. I first wrote and read this collection's titular poem, "Enigma," for Feminist Voices. So thank you, Audrey, thank you.

Thank you to Tumblr and to the AOK Podcast for helping me find the words.

Thank you to everyone who has ever left a comment on my social media posts or my fanfics saying things like, "That's exactly how it is for me! Thank you for putting it into words!" or, "This helped me figure out my identity. Thank you." You remind me that I'm doing what I'm supposed to be doing.

And finally – thank you, dear reader, for listening.

# Publication History

"Enigma" originally appeared in *Tell Magazine*, an online publication produced by the University of Iowa Department of Gender, Women's, and Sexuality Studies, 2018.

"Nothing and Everything" originally appeared in *Monologues by LGBTQIA+ Writers for LGBTQIA+ Actors*, a *some scripts* anthology, edited by Alyssa Cokinis, 2023.

The following works originally appeared on Instagram: "Again," "Commitment," "Coyotes," "Dimensions of Love," "Ever After," "Faults," "Forgive Me," "Goodnight Is Not Goodbye," "I Am Whole," "I Am Yours," "I Claim the Right," "I Have...," "Kintsugi," "Labels," "Leaving," "Missing You," "Perhaps I Cannot Keep You Warm," "Possible Love," "Queering," "The Tree Is Loved," "This Hand Is Yours," "To Be Loved," "To Be Seen," "Too Good," "Us," and "Who Raises the Dead."

The following works originally appeared on DailyPrompt: "Around My Heart," "Comets," "Date More," "Enchained," "Friendship," "Gardening," "HeartBroke," "Moonlight," "No Longer Do," "Promises," "Starlight," "To Not Believe," "We Fly," "Wedding Vows," and "You Never Asked, But..."

The following works originally appeared on TikTok: "Four-Letter Words," "Good, Valid, Important," "Love Song," "Out of Love," and "Self-Immolation."

All works have been revised for this publication.

# About the Author

Sophie A. Katz (she/her) is a queer, Jewish writer with a lot on her mind. A lifelong storyteller, Katz has a Master of Arts degree in Professional Creative Writing, and she currently writes shows for Disney parks, resorts, and cruise ships. She's also the host of the podcast, "I Love This Thing So Fricking Much." Katz identifies as greyromantic and demisexual, or simply "aro-ace."

Find out more at her website,
https://www.sophie-a-katz.com/,
or at @sophieakatz on Instagram, TikTok, and Tumblr.

For business inquiries, please contact her at
sophie.a.katz@gmail.com.